SIX ANTHEMS

DAVID GOODE AND FRANCIS WARNER

Together with a CD of these works
sung by the Choir of King's College, Cambridge,
conducted by Stephen Cleobury during Chapel Services

2014

The publisher wishes to express gratitude and place on record that this publication and these recordings have been made possible by generous grants over ten years from a husband and wife who wish to remain anonymous.

Text prepared by Alison Wiblin
Music prepared by Tom Recknell

In the accompanying CD the brass players performing with King's College Choir in *Anthem for Christ the King* were: trumpets – Christian Barraclough, Shane Brennan, and Toby Street; trombones – Barnaby Philpott and Rupert Whitehead. It was recorded during Evensong, 20 November 2011.

ISBN 978-0-86140-489-6

First published in 2014
by Colin Smythe Limited
38 Mill Lane
Gerrards Cross
Buckinghamshire SL9 8BA
www.colinsmythe.co.uk

FOR ANNE GOODE

1931–2004

CONTENTS

CD: Stephen Cleobury conducting the Choir of King's College, Cambridge.

David Goode at the organ of School Hall, Eton

© Graham Keutenius

Stephen Cleobury at the organ of King's College, Cambridge

© Nick Rutter

Francis Warner on tour in the USA, as a guest at the organ of Westminster College, Fulton, Missouri

© Darlene Johnson, USA

SIX ANTHEMS

This book is the outcome of over a decade's collaboration between three friends: David Goode as composer, Francis Warner as librettist, and Stephen Cleobury as choirmaster.

DAVID GOODE, M.A., M.PHIL., born 1971, composer and organist, combines a concert career that takes him round the world with being Organist of Eton College, where as a boy he was a music scholar and where his work includes teaching composition. From Eton he became Organ Scholar at King's College, Cambridge, 1991–1994, winning a double First Class Degree in Music, and taking the M.Phil in Musicology; then Sub-Organist at Christ Church, Oxford. He won the top prizes awarded at the 1997 St Albans Interpretation Competition, and the Recital Gold Medal at the 1998 Calgary Competition. From 2003–2005 he combined his busy international recital career with the post of Organist-in-Residence at First Congregational Church, Los Angeles, USA, home to the world's largest church organ. A frequent performer at the B.B.C. Promenade Concerts, where he has been a Featured Artist, he has made many recordings.

His compositions include work for the Los Angeles Philharmonic Orchestra, and his *Concert Fantasy on Themes by Gershwin* written for the new organ of Symphony Hall, Birmingham. His most recent is his setting of Francis Warner's *Blitz Requiem* for performance by the Bach Choir and Royal Philharmonic Orchestra in St Paul's Cathedral, London, September 2013, commemorating the 70th anniversary of the Blitz and the subsequent five years aerial bombardment of the British Isles.

STEPHEN CLEOBURY, C.B.E., M.A., MUS.B., HON D. MUS., HON F.R.C.M., F.R.C.O., F.R.S.C.M., born 1948, has since 1982 been Fellow, Organist and Director of Music at King's College, Cambridge, where he conducts the choir.

He is also Chorus Director of the Cambridge University Musical Society, University Organist, and Conductor Laureate of the BBC Singers. A past President of the Cathedral Organists' Association, he has also been President of the Royal College of Organists.

FRANCIS WARNER, M.A., D. LITT., HON D. MUS., born 1937, is Emeritus Fellow of St Peter's College, Oxford, and Residential Honorary Fellow of St Catharine's College, Cambridge, where in the 1950s he was a Choral Exhibitioner. Educated at Christ's Hospital and the London College of Music, at Cambridge he conducted his own re-scoring of Honegger's *King David* in King's College Chapel for two performances in 1958. In 2003 the recording of this concert was re-issued as a Landmark Recording CD by OxRecs Digital (OXCD–94).

Sixteen of his plays, his *Collected Poems 1960–1984*, *Nightingales: Poems 1985–1996*, and *By the Cam and the Isis* 1954–2000 (two long poems) are published by Colin Smythe Ltd, who also publishes *Blitz Requiem* by David Goode and Francis Warner in Conductor's Score, Full Score and Vocal Score.

Anthem for All Saints' Day

(FRANCIS WARNER)

SATB
& organ

DAVID GOODE

First performances given by the Choir of Eton College in Eton College Chapel
on the Eve of All Saints' Day, Friday 31st October conducted by Ralph Allwood
(Organist: Ben-San Lau), and by the Choir of St John's College, Cambridge in
St John's College Chapel on Saturday 1st November 2008 conducted by Andrew
Nethsingha (Organist: John Challenger)

Anthem for All Saints' Day

Gather my saints together unto me,
    Both old and new,
From jungle, ice-cap, bring their harvest through
    Christ's victory.

Call in all saints that cruelty still scorches,
    Strong through the Paraclete;
Round the arena burning as tar-torches;
    In, as live leopard-meat:

Priest who exchanged names to save one molest
    In ghetto's mass;
Mothers who press their infant to their breast
    From poisoning gas;

Souls who in time live by the values of
    Eternity,
Strengthened through suffering by sinews of
    Integrity,

Reap your reward where Eden's garden waits,
    Your freedom won
From pain. Now flowering joy for you creates
    A garland round the sun

While angels and archangels, and your friends
    Roll out the sky
In a red carpet where my rainbow bends
    To cradle your birth-cry.

Anthem for All Saints' Day

FRANCIS WARNER

DAVID GOODE

2

8

-to-ry.

to-ry.

ry.

ry.

ry.

Strong through the Pa - ra - clete;

Strong through the

Strong through the Pa - ra - clete;

Strong through the

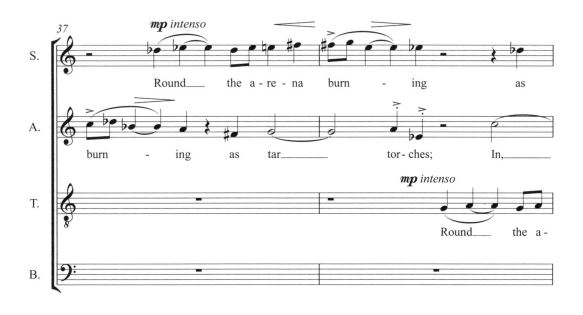

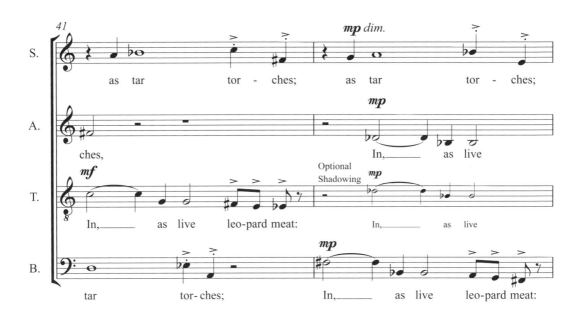

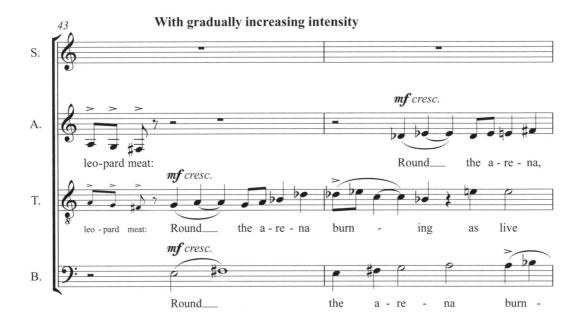

With gradually increasing intensity

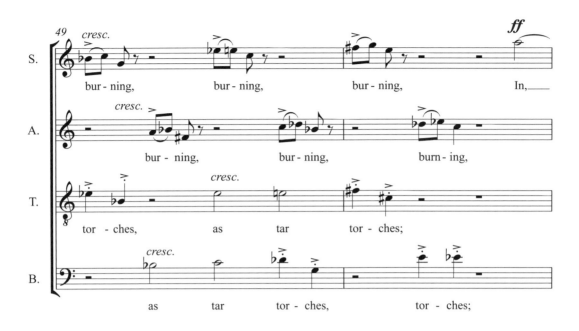

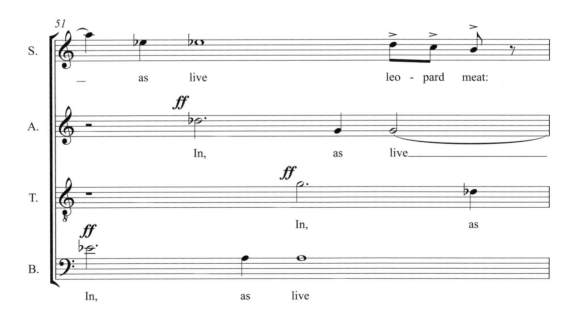

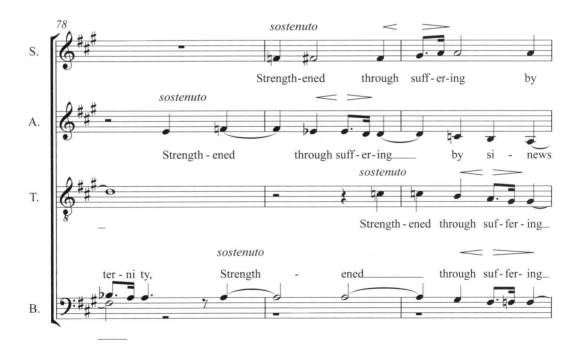

26

While an - gels and arch - an - gels, ___

Come prima

42

Anthem for St Catharine's Day

(FRANCIS WARNER)

SATB
& organ

DAVID GOODE

First performance given by the Choir of St Catharine's College, Cambridge in St Catharine's to celebrate the tercentenary of the consecration of the Chapel, St Catharine's Day, 25th November 2005 conducted by Edward Wickham (Organist: Matthew Cook)

Anthem for St Catharine's Day

Pass me a match, my son, to spin this torture,
 Spark the dark circle into furious light,
Scatter her fear of worst pain that can scorch her –
 Catharine, Bride of the Christ Child, girls' hoped sight,

Queen of all scholars, sleeping on Mount Moses –
 As she relives the Emperor's decree.
Death by dislimbing on the wheel exposes
 Horror of what's to come before we're free.

Words are the feathered pen that carves our thinking
 In blood on granite while we still have breath.
Pray in that numbness broken only by terror.
 Time is God's mercy that heals pain in death.

Still she destroys the wheel of human dreading,
 Blindness and ache of solitary hearts.
Victory triumphs over her beheading.
 Christ in His pity lifts the severed parts,

But in a new dimension, to His glory.
 Grace gave her courage when God's thunder came.
Now she is honoured in eternal story,
 And the great Cambridge college of her name,

As in a thousand thousand of her children,
 Church and cathedral, headland, mount, and sea.
Deathless at axe-stroke, she makes weak hearts quicken
 Living to praise Christ to eternity.

Anthem for St Catharine's Day

FRANCIS WARNER   DAVID GOODE

6

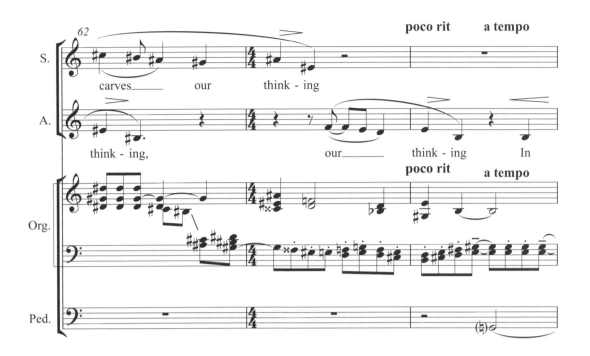

12

14

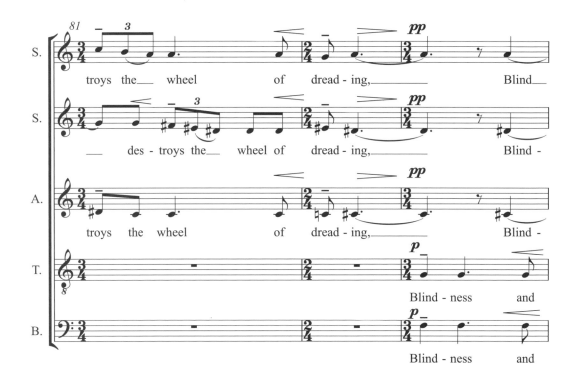

16

18

24

26

34

Anthem for St Cecilia's Day

(FRANCIS WARNER)

SATB
& organ

DAVID GOODE

First performance given by the Choir of King's College, Cambridge, in
King's College Chapel on the Eve of St Cecilia's Day, Sunday 21st November,
2004 conducted by Stephen Cleobury (Organist: Tom Winpenny)

Anthem for St Cecilia's Day

Shall I tell you what happens after death?
You want to know? Then down upon your knees
As these are serious and breathless thoughts,
Honey to ease your angel's song of woe.
Weep till black, lead tears lighten to rainbow
The starry vault of limping time, and melt
Transparent melodies of unheard notes,
Dear diapason; our felt, dancing hopes
Find Truth relent and beckon us beyond.

And from that angel choir one will come down
To welcome you, provided you will sing,
Praise the Creator from your broken heart,
Try out each instrument she offers: harp,
Shrill tambourine, or double bass, or flute,
Oboe, or melting 'cello's perfect tone,
The soaring trumpet's gold authority
Waking the trombone and bassoon; best, last,
Her own toccata'd organ's queenly bliss.

You lose your shadow, turning into flame.
Laughter and grief mutate to loud and soft.
Time becomes tempo, touch sheds into notes,
Speech into song, affection harmony.
Memory's plainsong lifts to counterpoint,
Darkness to dawn as she heals your blind eyes,
Discontent to delight's resolved discord.
Antiphonally war and peace exchange
Decani with cantoris, blessèd change.

Look! What on earth we thought were cherubs are
Simply God's grace-notes tip-circling his baton.
Our fear of change turns round into desire
For metamorphosis we've undergone
In a ground bass of gratitude to Him
Who when on earth, before his sacrifice,
Sang 'Tonus Peregrinus', that last hymn,
For sending us Cecilia, echoing
Our fresh-born souls tuned now for Paradise.

Anthem for St Cecilia's Day

for SATB & organ

FRANCIS WARNER

DAVID GOODE

A tempo **Senza rall.**

poco accel.

cresc.

- ney to ease your an-gel's song of woe.

Gt. + 4'.
Sw. + mixt.

Gt. to Ped.

Solo **f** *mf* *mp* *cresc.*

Weep, till black, lead tears____ tears_____ light - en to

Shut Sw.
Gt. 8' only

Reduce Sw. to 2', ob.

mp

Sw. to Ped. only

Find Truth, re - lent and bec - kon us, and

bec - kon us be - yond.

And from that an - gel

And from that an - gel

And from that an - gel

And from that an - gel

6

12

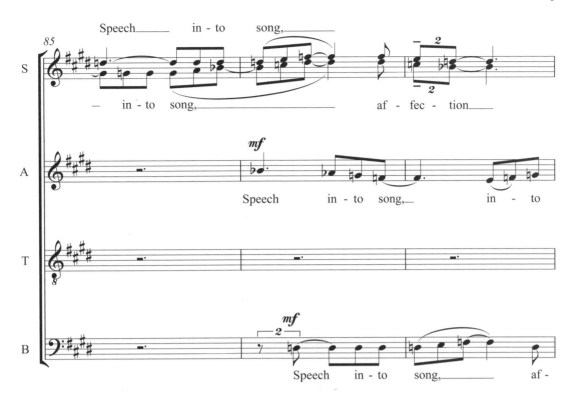

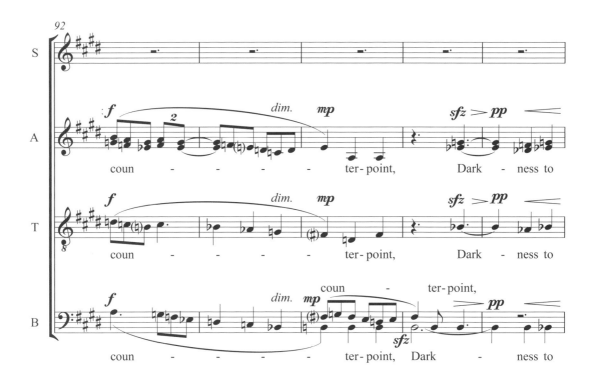

20

Anthem for St Peter's Day

(FRANCIS WARNER)

SATB
& organ

DAVID GOODE

First performance given by the Choir of St Peter's College, Oxford, on St Peter's Day, 29th June 2007 in Liverpool Cathedral conducted by Rory McCleery (Organist: Jonathan Lo)

Anthem for St Peter's Day

'Will you leave everything and come with me –
Yes, bring your brother, leave the nets and sea,
            And fish for human souls?'
    'The mother of my wife is ill.'
    'Her raging fever I will still
            Before this high sun rolls
    Behind those hills.' 'We trust your nod,
    Jesus, Son of the Living God.'

    'Blessèd are you, Simon, for this!
    My heavenly Father in his bliss
            Opens your eyes.
    I call you Peter now, the rock
    On which my church will stand all shock.
            You hold the keys
    To bind or loose, in heaven, on earth.
    Have faith, as I have in your worth.'

    The High Priest's maid said: 'Galilean
    Warming your hands, that prisoner's friend…'
            'He's not my friend.'
    Another pointed: 'He's one of them!'
            'Girl, you offend!'
    A Roman sneered: 'You share his accent.'
    'I resent and I condemn
Inept lies!' The cock crowed. Peter wept.

    They dined deep. Risen Christ bent down
    To wash their feet, to Peter's frown.
    'Simon, John's son, do you love me?'
            'Yes, Lord, I do.'
    'Simon, John's son, do you love me?'
            'You know I do!'
    'Simon, John's son, do you love me?
            Feed my sheep.

    When you were young your ways were free.
    When you are old you'll follow me
            With outstretched hands.'
    And so it was. Agrippa tried
    Peter as godless; crucified
            As Rome commands –
But upside-down, the martyr's own request
Lest he should equal Jesus ever blest.

Anthem for St Peter's Day

FRANCIS WARNER

DAVID GOODE

'Will you leave ev-ery-thing_____ and come with me–

Yes,___ bring your bro-ther, leave___ the nets and sea, And

2

fish_____ for hu - man souls?'

'Her rag - ing fe - ver___ I will still___

'The moth - er of my wife is ill.'

4

A tempo, ma espansivo ♩ = 58

'Bles - sed are you, Sim - on, for this!
'Bles - sed are you, Sim - on,
'Bles - sed are you, Sim- on, for this!
'Bles - - sed are you, for

My heaven-ly Fa - ther in his bliss Op-ens your eyes. I call you
for this! My Fa-ther in his bliss Op-ens your eyes. I call you
My heaven-ly Fa-ther in his bliss Op-ens your eyes. I call you
this! In bliss Op - ens your eyes. I call you

6

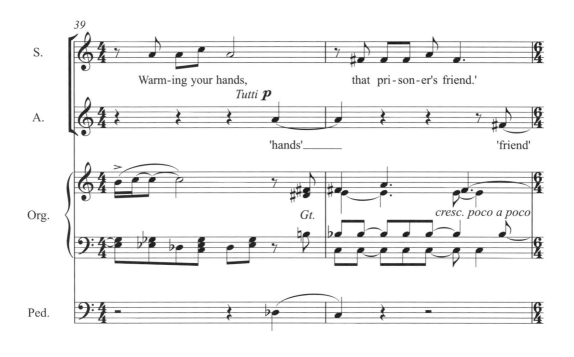

12

14

20

[146]

Anthem for the Visitation

(FRANCIS WARNER)

SATB
a cappella

DAVID GOODE

First performance given by the Choir of Christ Church Cathedral in Christ
Church, Oxford, on the Feast of the Visitation of the Blessed Virgin Mary,
Thursday 2nd July, 2009 conducted by Clive Driskill-Smith.

Anthem for the Visitation

Elisabeth   I'm an old woman
          Breeding a child
That leaps like a lion
          Prowling the wild.
How will I cope
          When my time comes?
A young pair of hands
          Not an old pair of gums
Is my need and my hope.

Mary   I am a young girl
          Under a cloud
Pregnant not married
          Blamed but unbowed,
Rose with no garden
          Under the sky.
Cousin, I'll help you,
Bathe the young whelp too,
          At his first cry.

Elisabeth   There! Did you see him
          Kick in the womb
Just as you spoke? A hymn
          Sing to God whom
We are trusting, who blesses you,
          Queen of my Lord.
When pain oppresses you
Jesus possesses you;
          Be reassured.

Mary   I delight in my Saviour
       Lifting me up
   From nothing till men bless
       Me, wine in the cup.
   His mercy and strength
       Tame the proud, feed the poor.
   As he told to our prophet,
   He comes as our forfeit
       To prove love secure.

Elisabeth Nothing's impossible,
       God can do all.
   I don't deserve
       Such a joy to enthral:
   Enemies cease
       As his dayspring on high
   Dispelling the dark
       Like a lark with its cry
   Comes to guide us to peace.

Mary   As Gabriel urged me
       I hurried and found
   You here with your husband.
       Time is turned round.
   You hide hope that's fragrant,
       Five months as you grow
   Here, where Juda is hilly;
   New leaf on the lily,
       First crocus through snow.

Anthem for the Visitation

FRANCIS WARNER

DAVID GOODE

6

8

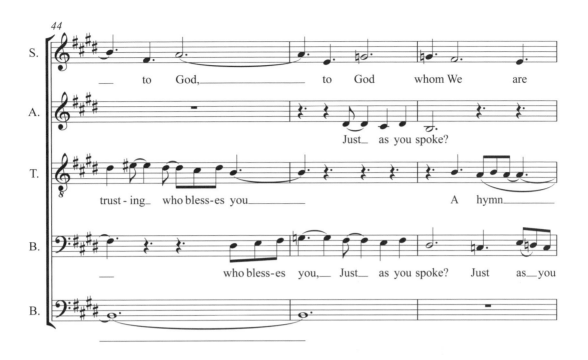

10

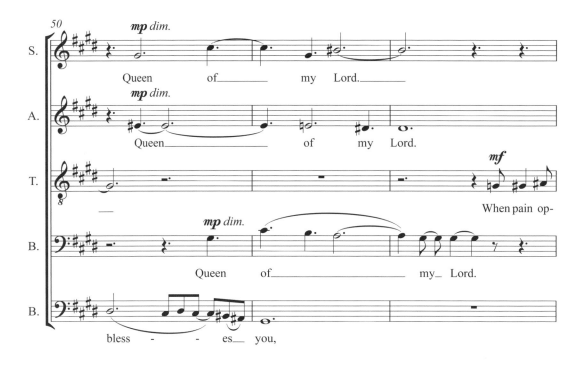

12

14

20

22

molto rit.   a tempo

[178]

rit. al fine

Anthem for Christ the King

(FRANCIS WARNER)

SATB, 3 trumpets,
2 trombones, and organ

DAVID GOODE

First performance given by the Choir of King's College, Cambridge, together with members of Prime Brass, in King's College Chapel on Saturday 21st November 2009, the Eve of the Feast of Christ the King, conducted by Stephen Cleobury (Organist: Peter Stevens)

Anthem for Christ the King

Not in a crown of gold but with the stars,
With oceans as his coronation drums,
Not in a crown of thorns but lightning's wars
The maker of the universe, Christ comes.
Yet to the heart of suffering he plumbs.
The past torments us, what's to come dismays.
His understanding pity draws our praise.

The resurrected Christ, King of Creation,
Whose flags are branches, coach a donkey's trot,
Who fills relationships with love's elation,
Who chose straw in a stable for his cot,
Answers our anguish as our bodies rot:
'Lord, in your kingdom reach us through our vice!'
'Today you'll be with me in Paradise.'

He turns our royal pageants upside-down,
Subverts earth's power structures into dust.
Blest bride and bridegroom close the General's frown,
For dew of youth lasts not by laws but trust,
And open homes dissolve the beggar's crust.
The margin is the centre. Losing all,
We find grace comes back like a waterfall.

Magnificence, ruler of seas and shores,
Music and joy of life, whose flaming force
Turned timid men into world conquerors,
Your spirit's light reflects back to its source,
Praying within us, healing our remorse.
Come Holy Trinity, your kingdom won:
Lover, belov'd, and love itself, in one.

Anthem for Christ the King

FRANCIS WARNER

DAVID GOODE

6

8

Christ comes.

Christ comes.

Christ comes.

Christ comes.

dim.

dim.

12

14

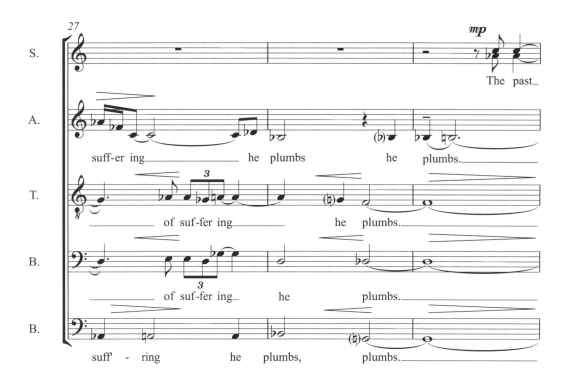

22

Poco con moto

24

28

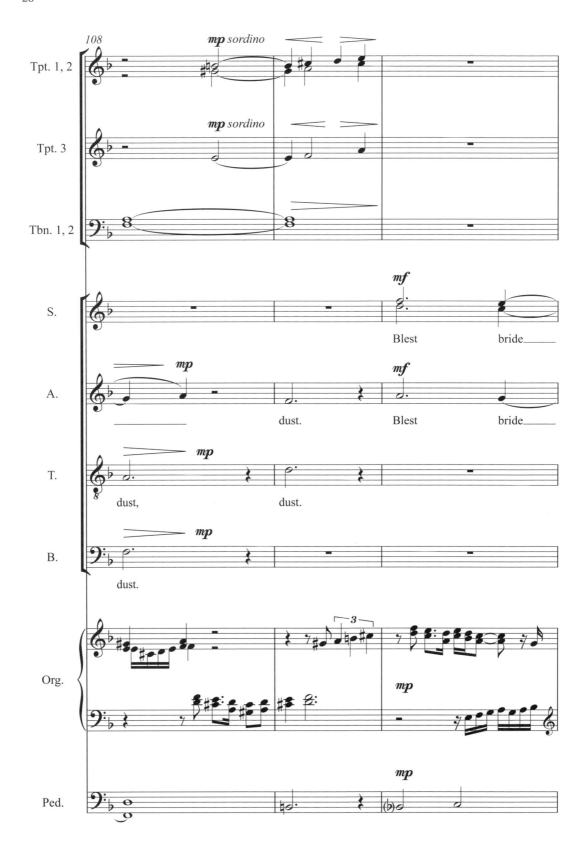

32

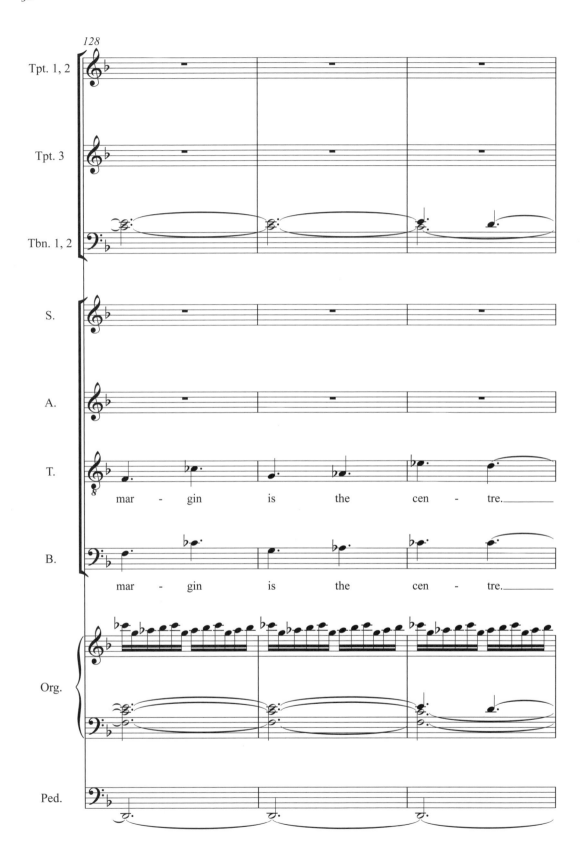

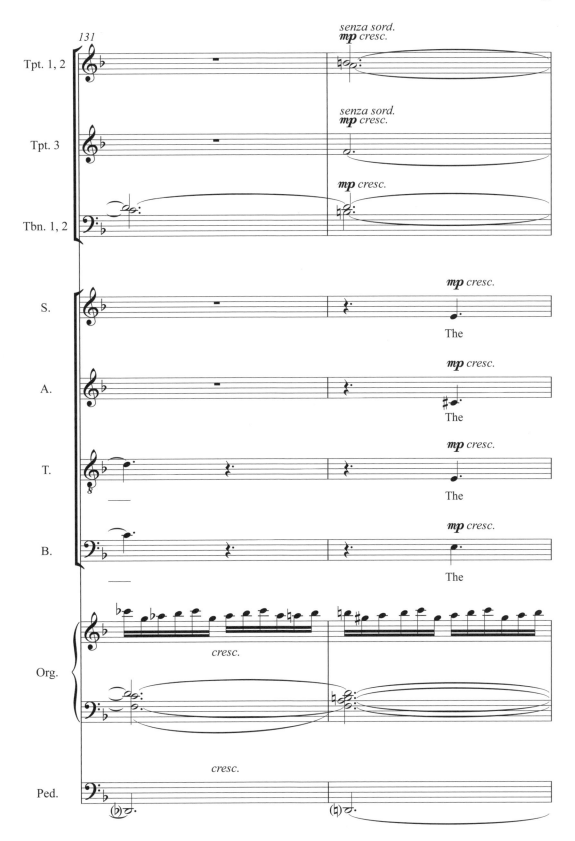

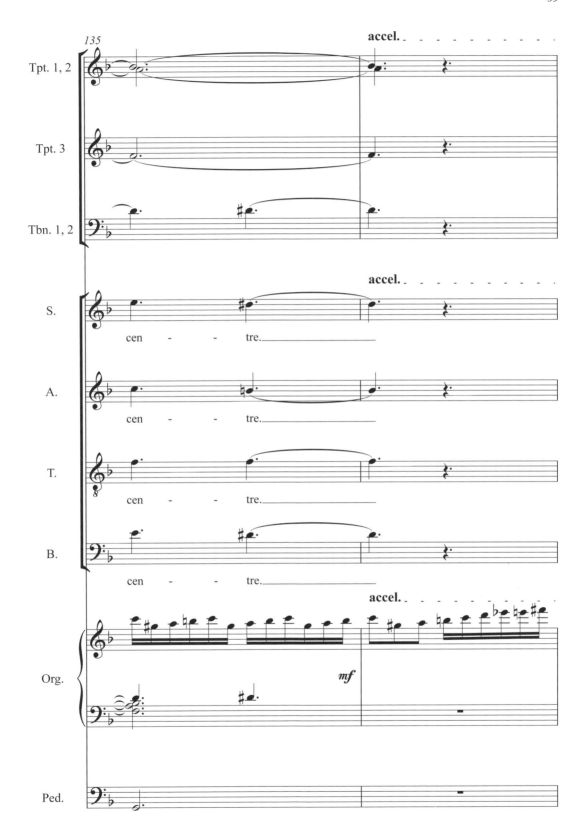

36

Come prima ma slargando

42

52

Variations on a Theme by Francis Warner

(ORGAN)

Solo version

DAVID GOODE

Composed for the Cambridge Summer Music Festival 2007
and first performed by David Goode
on the organ of King's College Chapel
Wednesday, 25 July 2007

The concert was sponsored by Cambridge University Press

This work is playable either as a solo, or a duet. The duet features in each variation a harder and and easier part, and variations can be allocated between any number of players.

An earlier version was performed by the composer and several students in Eton College Chapel on June 10th 2007.

Variations on a Theme by Francis Warner

SOLO VERSION

DAVID GOODE

2

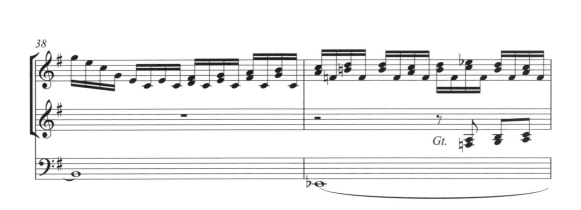

4

Tres lent

Gt. flute harmonique 8'

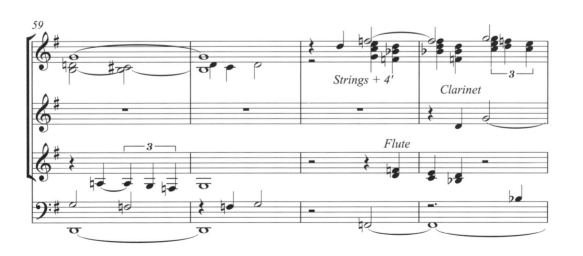

8

Adagio espressivo (nobilmente)

Ch. and Sw. foundations 8' coupled

Gt foundations 8' (Ch. Sw. coupled)

Ped. foundations 16' 8' Sw. coupled

Ch.

soft foundations only

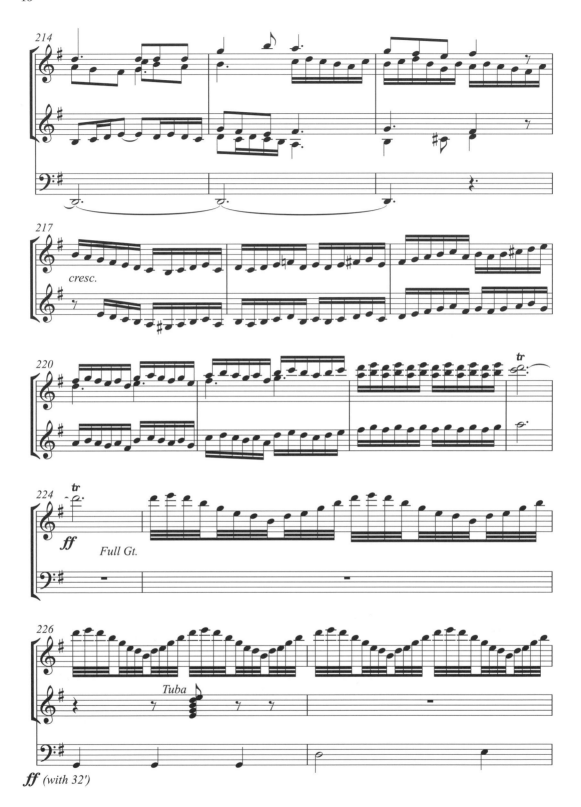

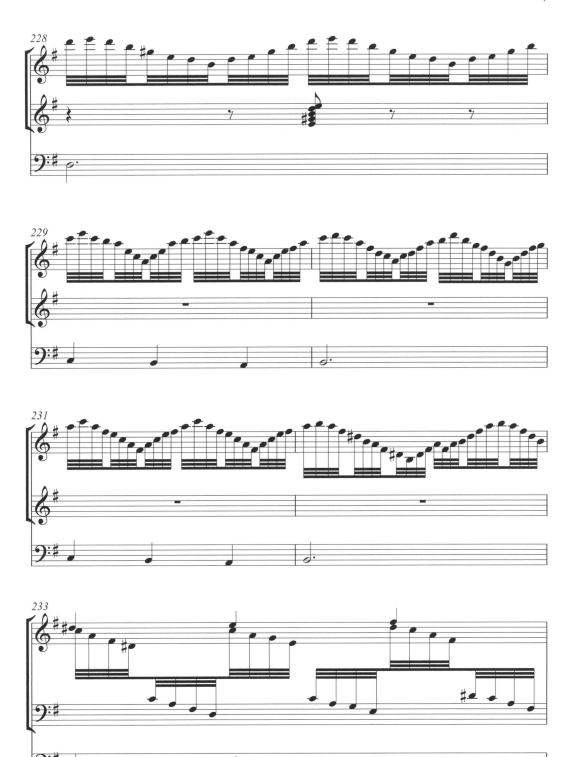

18

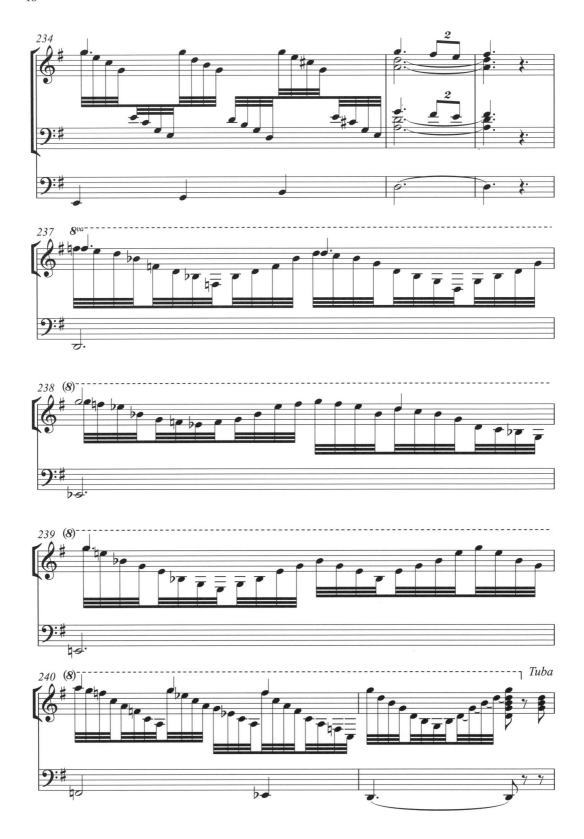

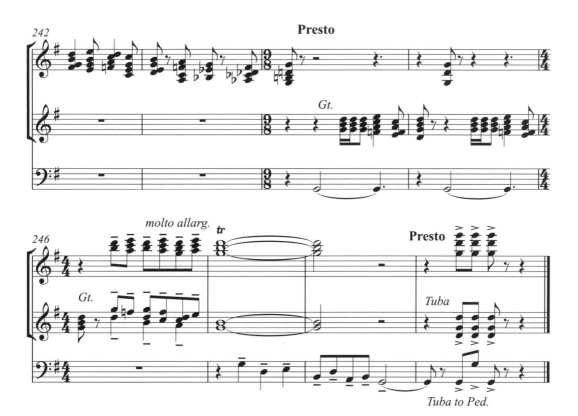

Variations on a Theme by Francis Warner

DUET VERSION

DAVID GOODE

2

Grandioso e marcato
(♩ = 69)

Piu mosso, risoluto (♩ = 90)
Choir 8'4'
Full Swell (shut) coupled

16' 8' Sw. coupled

Gt.

4

6

12

Adagio espressivo (nobilmente)

14

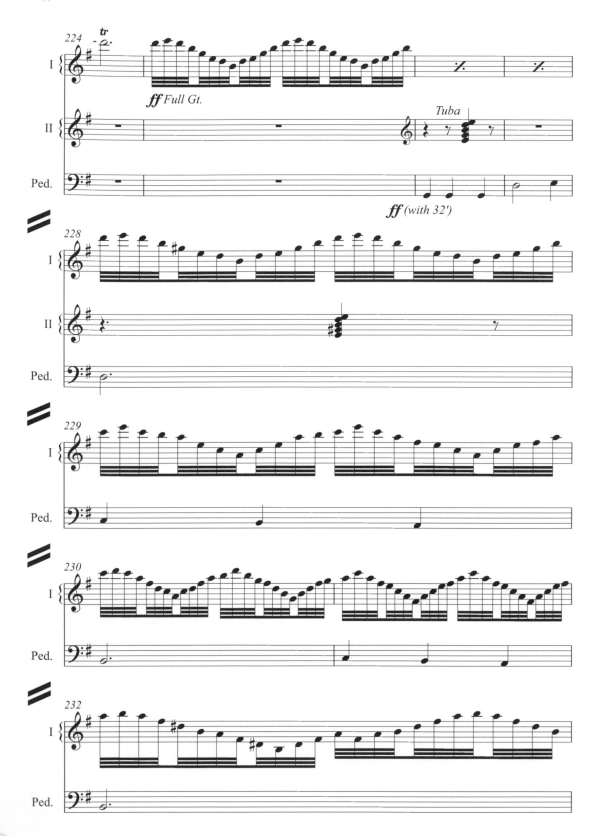

20

[278]